Instant Nokogiri

Learning data scraping and parsing in Ruby using the
Nokogiri gem

Hunter Powers

BIRMINGHAM - MUMBAI

Instant Nokogiri

Copyright © 2013 Packt Publishing

First published: August 2013

Production Reference: 1240813

Published by Packt Publishing Ltd.
Livery Place
35 Livery Street
Birmingham B3 2PB, UK.

ISBN 978-1-78328-997-4

www.packtpub.com

Credits

Author

Hunter Powers

Reviewer

Eduardo Figarola Mota

Acquisition Editor

Kunal Parikh

Commissioning Editor

Govindan K.

Technical Editor

Sonali S. Vernekar

Project Coordinator

Sherin Padayatty

Proofreader

Kelly Hutchinson

Production Coordinator

Kyle Albuquerque

Cover Work

Kyle Albuquerque

Cover Image

Abhinash Sahu

About the Author

Hunter Powers, a Full Stack web developer, began programming at the age of 6 and has been gathering steam ever since. From childhood awards (including "Most Outstanding Presentation in the Field of Engineering" from NC State University and "Superior Achievement in Computer Science" from the North Carolina Student Academy of Science) to more recent achievements at TechCrunch Disrupt 2012, he has never lost his passion for the science, languages, and dynamics of computers. His early accomplishments in the field led him to open WireThePlanet.com, his first business, at the age of 13. The company has prospered through the years, developing local and national websites, producing national television advertisements, and directing the art and design for an international card and print company. With a range of products such as websites, book covers, advertising, logos, and national festivals, his customer base includes e-commerce companies, charities and clubs, renowned foodies, and even the weatherman.

In 2011, Powers joined a big data streaming company. His work there has been represented by projects for AOL's TechCrunch, Engadget, The Washington Post, The New York Times, Fox's X-Factor, Fox Sports Australia, New York Presbyterian Hospital, and The NFL, to name a few.

A graduate of The University of Virginia, Powers interests extend beyond technology into filmmaking, photography, and writing. He was first published while in high school in 4 *Guys from Rolla* and has written many short, as well as a feature length, science fiction and screenplays. Powers also directs with credits for multiple commercial, web videos, and short films.

Currently residing in the Logan Circle arts district in Washington, DC, Powers is working on his next book. You can find his blog at `http://www.HunterPowers.com`.

About the Reviewer

Eduardo Figarola Mota graduated from the Universidad de Colima with a degree in software engineering. Deeply entrenched in web technologies, he loves programming, and Ruby has become his favorite language.

Currently working for Crowd Interactive, a leading Ruby on Rails consultancy in Mexico, Eduardo finds himself surrounded with cutting-edge technology and Mexico's greatest programming talent.

This is Eduardo's first book serving as Reviewer.

I'd like to thank my friends, family, and girlfriend for the continuous support.

www.packtpub.com

Support files, eBooks, discount offers, and more

You might want to visit www.packtpub.com for support files and downloads related to your book.

Did you know that Packt offers eBook versions of every book published, with PDF and ePub files available? You can upgrade to the eBook version at www.packtpub.com and as a print book customer, you are entitled to a discount on the eBook copy. Get in touch with us at service@packtpub.com for more details.

At www.packtpub.com, you can also read a collection of free technical articles, sign up for a range of free newsletters and receive exclusive discounts and offers on Packt books and eBooks.

packtlib.packtpub.com

Do you need instant solutions to your IT questions? PacktLib is Packt's online digital book library. Here, you can access, read and search across Packt's entire library of books.

Why Subscribe?

- ✦ Fully searchable across every book published by Packt
- ✦ Copy and paste, print and bookmark content
- ✦ On demand and accessible via web browser

Free Access for Packt account holders

If you have an account with Packt at www.packtpub.com, you can use this to access PacktLib today and view nine entirely free books. Simply use your login credentials for immediate access.

Table of Contents

Instant Nokogiri

Welcome to *Instant Nokogiri*. This book has been especially created to provide you with all the information that you need to get set up with Nokogiri. You will learn the basics of Nokogiri, get started with building your first app, and discover some tips and tricks for using Nokogiri.

This book contains the following sections:

So, what is Nokogiri? helps you find out what Nokogiri actually is, what you can do with it, and why it's so great.

Installation explains how to download and install Nokogiri with minimum fuss and then set it up so that you can use it as soon as possible.

Quick start – creating your first Nokogiri application will guide you through the creation of your first Nokogiri app. You will identify content, extract just the right parts, and incorporate the new data using the Nokogiri gem.

Top 13 features you need to know about explains how to integrate the most common Nokogiri methods with your Ruby code, along with a few tips and tricks. By the end of this section you will be able to scrape and parse disparate data sources with ease.

People and places you should get to know provides you with many useful links to the project page and forums, as well as a number of helpful articles, tutorials, and the Twitter feeds of Nokogiri super-contributors.

So, what is Nokogiri?

Nokogiri (htpp://nokogiri.org/) is the most popular open source Ruby gem for HTML and XML parsing. It parses HTML and XML documents into node sets and allows for searching with CSS3 and XPath selectors. It may also be used to construct new HTML and XML objects.

The Nokogiri homepage is shown in the following screenshot:

Nokogiri is fast and efficient. It combines the raw power of the native C parser Libxml2 (http://www.xmlsoft.org/) with the intuitive parsing API of Hpricot (https://github.com/hpricot/hpricot).

The primary use case for a parsing library is data scraping. Data scraping is the process of extracting data intended for humans and structuring it for input into another program. Data by itself is meaningless without structure. Software imposes rigid structure over data referred to as format.

The same can be said of spoken language. We do not yell out random sounds and expect them to have meaning. We use words to form sentences to form meaning. This is our format. It is a loose structure. You could learn ten words in a foreign language, combine those with a few hand symbols, and add in a little amateur acting to convey fairly advanced concepts to people who don't speak your native tongue. This interpretive prowess is not shared by computers. Computer communication must follow protocols; fail to follow the protocol and no communication will be made.

The goal here is to bridge the two. Take the data intended for humans, get rid of the superfluous, and parse it into a structured data format for a computer. Data intended for humans is inherently fickle as the structure frequently changes. Data scraping should be used as a last effort and is generally appropriate in two scenarios: interfacing systems with incompatible data formats, and third-party sources lacking an API. If you aren't solving one of these two problems, you probably shouldn't be scraping.

An example of this is the most common scrape and parse use case in tutorials on the Internet: Amazon price searching. The scenario is: you have a database of products and you want up-to-date pricing information. The tutorials inevitably lead you through the process of scraping and parsing Amazon's search results to extract prices. The problem is, Amazon provides an API with all of this information and more on the Amazon Product Advertising API.

It is important to remember that you are using someone else's server resources when scraping. This is why the preferred method of accessing information should always be a developer approved API. An API in general will provide faster, cleaner, and more direct access to data while not expressing undue toll on the provider's servers.

A wealth of information sits waiting on the Internet. A small fraction is made easily accessible to developers via APIs. Nokogiri bridges that gap with its slick, fast, HTML and XML parsing engine bundled in an easy to use Ruby gem.

Installation

In the following five easy steps we will install Nokogiri, along with all required dependencies and verify everything is working.

Development environments are very idiosyncratic and developers are notorious for spending excess time tweaking every aspect. The boss regularly proclaims, "I don't want you spending all day crafting some bash script that saves you 10 minutes". But it's in our nature; we make things and then we make them better.

The following are the tools we use everyday to craft software. If you know enough to use something else, go right ahead. If you want to skip something, feel a different version is better, or doubt the need for a requirement, do it. But if you're just getting started, follow along as closely as possible for the best experience.

Step 1 – what do I need?

The requirements are as follows:

+ Ruby version 1.9.2 or greater
+ RubyGems
+ Nokogiri Gem
+ Bundler Gem
+ Text editor or Ruby IDE
+ Terminal
+ Google Chrome

Ruby, RubyGems, and the specific gems are hard requirements. The text editor or IDE, terminal, and browser are more personal preference. Here are a few good ones:

+ Ruby Mine (`http://www.jetbrains.com/ruby/`) is the premier cross-platform IDE for Ruby development. It is a commercial product and well admired in the Ruby community. However, most Ruby developers prefer a raw text editor over a full IDE experience.

+ Sublime Text 2 (`http://www.sublimetext.com/`) is an excellent cross-platform text editor that is well suited for a variety of languages, including Ruby. While it is also a commercial product, you can try it out via a full feature never expiring demo.

In OS X, the native terminal `Terminal.app` is fine. (Go to **Applications** | **Utilities** | **Terminal. app**.) For some additional power, split pane, and tab support, download the free **iTerm2** from `http://www.iterm2.com/`. On Linux, the default terminal is fine. Windows users, see the end of the section, *Step 3 – RubyGems*, for a quick run through of your options.

Step 2 – Ruby

Nokogiri requires Ruby version 1.9.2 or greater. To check your version of Ruby, enter on the command line:

```
$ ruby -v
ruby 1.8.7 (2012-02-08 patchlevel 358) [universal-darwin12.0
```

If the number after Ruby in the response is 1.9.2 or greater then skip to *Step 3 – RubyGems*.

In this example, a stock install of Mac OS X 10.8.4, we are running 1.8.7 and will need to upgrade.

In order to compile the necessary dependencies in OS X, you will need to install the developer tools. If you are running a Linux variant, you may omit this dependency. We will cover Windows in a short while.

If you are unsure whether you have previously installed developer tools, you can run gcc from the command line:

```
$ gcc
-bash: gcc: command not found
```

If you receive command not found, you can be certain that developer tools are not present.

Apple's free download page for developer utilities is shown in the following screenshot:

There are two options for OS X developer tools: XCode and command-line tools. XCode (`https://developer.apple.com/xcode/`) comes with a complete IDE and several OS X and iOS SDKs. None of these extras will assist you with your Ruby development and this install will run you a couple of gigs.

The recommended alternative is command-line tools (`https://developer.apple.com/downloads/`), which stays well under a gig. You will need a free Apple developer account to complete the download. When you are done, you can re-run the `gcc` command and receive a better response:

```
$ gcc
i686-apple-darwin11-llvm-gcc-4.2: no input files
```

Rather than directly installing the required Ruby version, we are going to install an interdependency: **Ruby Version Manager** (**RVM**) to manage our Ruby installation. RVM is an easy way to install and manage multiple versions of Ruby. As a Ruby developer, you will often find it necessary to keep multiple versions of Ruby on your system to fulfill various requirements.

The RVM homepage is shown in the following screenshot:

To install RVM run the following command:

```
$ curl -L https://get.rvm.io | bash -s stable --ruby=2.0.0
```

This will install Ruby, RubyGems, and take care of all dependencies. You may be prompted to enter your password during the installation. Once complete, restart your terminal, and you should be running Ruby 2.0.0. You can verify this from the command line by running:

```
$ ruby -v
ruby 2.0.0p195 (2013-05-14 revision 40734) [x86_64-darwin12.4.0]
```

You should now see Ruby 2.0.0 installed.

If you run into any issues installing RVM, you can run:

```
$ rvm requirements
```

to see what additional software is needed. If you already have RVM installed and only need to update Ruby you can run:

```
$ rvm install 2.0.0
```

Once installed, run:

```
$ rvm --use 2.0.0
```

to make use of the new version.

Step 3 – RubyGems

RubyGems solves two main problems in the Ruby ecosystem. First, it enables Ruby libraries to be bundled in a self-contained updatable format known as gems. Second it provides a server to manage the distribution and installation of these gems. RubyGems were likely installed as part of your Ruby installation, if you installed Ruby with RVM, and you can skip to the next step.

To check if RubyGems is installed, from the command line run:

```
$ gem
-bash: gem: command not found
```

If it is installed correctly, it should come back with a message. RubyGems is a sophisticated package manager for Ruby along with some help information. If you instead receive `command not found`, you will need to install RubyGems manually.

The RubyGems homepage on RubyForge is shown in the following screenshot:

Download the latest version of RubyGems from RubyForge (`http://rubyforge.org/frs/?group_id=126`), for example **rubygems-1.8.25.zip**. Decompress the archive, navigate to the folder in your terminal, and execute:

```
$ ruby setup.rb
```

You should now have RubyGems installed. Restart your terminal session and try running the `gem` command again, you should no longer see `command not found`:

```
$ gem
RubyGems is a sophisticated package manager for Ruby. This is a basic
help message containing pointers to more information.
```

Windows users, you have not been forgotten. Most Ruby developers on Windows develop in a **VM** (**Virtual Machine**). Windows lacks a good build system and has general compatibility issues with Ruby dependencies.

The free VirtualBox Windows-compatible VM homepage is shown in the following screenshot:

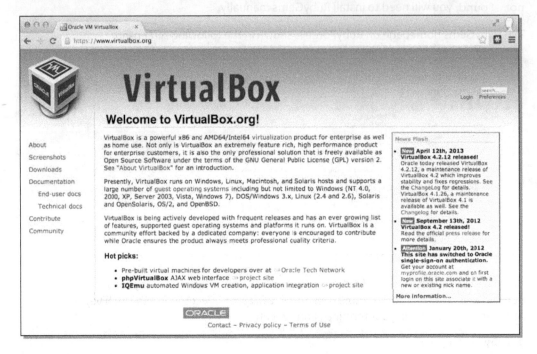

Installation and configuration of a virtual machine is outside the scope of this book. A good free virtualization system is VirtualBox (https://www.virtualbox.org/). A good free Linux OS to run on your virtualization system is Ubuntu (http://www.ubuntu.com/download/desktop). Packt Publishing has the excellent *VirtualBox: Beginner's Guide* (http://www.packtpub.com/virtualbox-3-1-beginners-guide), and Google is your friend.

If you're not quite ready to install a VM and wish to try and stay in a native Windows environment, download and install RailsInstaller (http://railsinstaller.org/) with Ruby 1.9.2 or greater. This will set up your system with Ruby, RubyGems, a command prompt, and a few other development dependencies. Once installed, skip to *Step 4 – Nokogiri and Bundler*.

Step 4 – Nokogiri and Bundler

Nokogiri and Bundler are Ruby gems. Bundler is the standard system for managing dependencies in Ruby projects. With the correct dependencies installed, their installation should be the easiest of them all. From the command line run:

```
$ gem install nokogiri
Successfully installed nokogiri-1.6.0
$ sudo gem install nokogiri
Successfully installed nokogiri-1.6.0
```

If you receive an error about permissions, you can prepend sudo to the commands and try again.

 Nokogori used to require a separate native install of Libxml2. With the 1.6.0 release, lead developer *Mike Dalessio* adopted a "Fat Gem" policy and started embedding the native libraries for different platforms within the gem.

Everything is installed and configured. Time to make sure everything is working.

Step 5 – verify

We are going to make sure everything is set up correctly and working with a quick code snippet. Open your preferred text editor and try out this sample, which should return the top Google results for Packt Publishing – the finest tech book publisher in the world!

```
# import nokogiri to parse and open-uri to scrape
require 'nokogiri'
require 'open-uri'

# set the URL to scape
url = 'http://www.google.com/search?q=packt'

# create a new Nokogiri HTML object from the scraped URL
doc = Nokogiri::HTML(open(url))

# loop through an array of objects matching a CSS selector
doc.css('h3.r').each do |link|
  # print the link text
  puts link.content
end
```

Downloading the example code

You can download the example code files for all Packt books you have purchased from your account at `http://www.packtpub.com`. If you purchased this book elsewhere, you can visit `http://www.packtpub.com/support` and register to have the files e-mailed directly to you.

Now execute the Ruby script and you should see the titles for the top results:

```
$ ruby google_results.rb
Packt Publishing: Home
Books
Latest Books
Login/register
PacktLib
Support
Contact
Packt - Wikipedia, the free encyclopedia
Packt Open Source (PacktOpenSource) on Twitter
Packt Publishing (packtpub) on Twitter
Packt Publishing | LinkedIn
Packt Publishing | Facebook
```

And that's it

Before proceeding, take a moment and look at the Ruby script. You may not understand everything that's going on, but you should be able to see the power we can pull from such a few lines of code. In the next section, we will break it all down and expose the thoughts behind each line as we craft our first Nokogiri-enabled application.

Quick start – creating your first Nokogiri application

For our first application, we are going to build the base for a news aggregation site. News aggregation sites, such as Drudge Report (http://www.drudgereport.com/), are both popular and profitable.

News aggregation sites rely on a human editor to cull top stories from around the web and link to them on their homepage. We are going to attempt to usurp the need for pesky humans and automate the selection of articles via data scraping and parsing.

We will focus on workflow as much as actual code. Workflow is of paramount importance, and by following these simple steps we will end up with cleaner, more concise, and maintainable code.

It's important to acknowledge that we are dealing with live data. By the time you read this, the top story will have changed and page structure may have changed with it, hence the importance of workflow. You need to be able to adapt to your data.

Step 1 – research

The first thing we need to do is identify our sources. For the sake of this quick start, we will limit this to one source. What if we could pull the top headline off The New York Times? Their website receives over 30 million unique visitors a month and does over 100 million in advertising a year. That should be a good start for our news aggregation site. The New York Times homepage is shown in the following screenshot:

Our goal is to parse the following two pieces of information off The New York Times homepage:

✦ The text for the top headline
✦ The URL that the top headline links to

With our goals in sight, it's time to turn our attention to the **Document Object Model (DOM)**. The DOM is the standard convention used for representing objects in HTML. Put a little simpler, the DOM is the HTML structure.

We need to determine the structure of the top news heading. Just by looking at the page, we can see that it has slightly larger text. This is promising, as it indicates it likely has its own CSS style. We can investigate further by inspecting the headline in Chrome Developer Tools. Right-click on the headline in Chrome and select **Inspect Element**. This will load the element inside the tools.

Viewing the source and inspecting the headline in Chrome is shown in the following screenshot:

Look at the HTML source; the top heading is wrapped inside an <a> anchor link tag within a <h2> heading:

```
<h2>
  <a href="http://www.nytimes.com/2013/06/10/us/former-cia-worker-
says-he-leaked-surveillance-data.html?hp">
  Ex-Worker at
  C.I.A. Says He
```

```
      Leaked Data on
      Surveillance</a>
    </h2>
```

Quickly scanning the remainder of the source, this appears to be the only <h2> present. This means we should not need a greater degree of specificity.

Our goal in analyzing the DOM is to determine a selector we can use to target the headline. The Nokogiri parser works by passing a selector and returning matched elements or nodes. Nokogiri supports two types of selectors: XPath and CSS.

XPath is a language designed for selecting nodes in an XML document. XPath works by representing an XML document as a tree that allows you to select nodes with different levels of specificity by navigating further and further down branches or nodes.

The XPath language looks a lot like the standard file path syntax in a *nix file system. The standard example XPATH selector is /A/B/C, where C is a child of B, which is a child of A. So you are selecting all C elements nested within B elements nested within A elements.

CSS is the language used to style HTML documents. CSS selectors are how one targets a part of the HTML document for styling. CSS selectors make use of a similar tree-like selection pattern with a few exceptions. HTML objects often contain a class or ID. In the case when you are using a class, you prepend the name with a period. In the case you are using an ID, you prepend the name of the ID with a hash mark.

Lucky for us, our goal is only to select the <a> anchor link inside the <h2> tag, which we believe to be the only one on the page.

+ The XPATH selector for this element is //h2/a
+ The CSS selector for this element is h2 a

We are going to use the CSS selector for this application as they are significantly faster to search for in Nokogiri. There is also a lot of additional selection power with the support for CSS3.

While the selections used in this application are very basic, if you would like to learn more about selectors, you can read the W3C CSS specification which contains the complete set of rules regarding valid CSS selectors http://www.w3.org/TR/CSS21/syndata.html#value-def-identifier.

> If you prefer a more visual approach to identifying selectors, try out the free Selector Gadget bookmarklet http://selectorgadget.com/. Selector Gadget allows you to click elements and instantly see CSS and XPath selectors.

Step 2 – explore

We now have a goal and a hypothesis about how we can reach that goal. Our hypothesis is that we can extract the headline for the top New York Times story by looking for the first <a> anchor link contained within the first and only <h2> heading.

We will use **IRB**, the interactive Ruby shell, to test our theory and explore coding strategies. IRB is an excellent way to play with new code and gems. If you have not used IRB before, it is a REPL that comes bundled with Ruby. A **read-eval-print loop** (**REPL**) is an interactive shell that allows you to enter an expression which is evaluated and the result displayed.

To launch the Ruby REPL IRB, simply type from the command line:

```
$ irb
```

This will launch and you should get back a prompt that looks something like:

```
2.0.0p195 :001 >
```

 For a slightly cleaner prompt try adding a `--simple-prompt` to IRB when launching.

The first thing we need to do is scrape the page. Scraping the page is a very easy task in Ruby. We will make use of **OpenURI** (`http://www.ruby-doc.org/stdlib-2.0/libdoc/open-uri/rdoc/OpenURI.html`), which is part of the Ruby Standard Library, meaning it comes bundled with Ruby. OpenURI makes it easy to open a URL as though it was a local file. We will need to import it with a require statement:

```
> require 'open-uri'
```

If this works successfully, we should receive a response of:

```
=> true
```

Now, we'll load the HTML source into a variable using OpenURI:

```
> data = open('http://nytimes.com')
```

Assuming a good network connection, this will return back `Tempfile` with the HTML source. It should look something like this:

```
=> #<Tempfile:/var/folders/19/2p_x8hqj4b737c401bpb99zw0000gn/T/open-
uri20130610-37901-xaavtx>
```

We can treat this new data object like any other file. For example, we can check that we successfully scraped the source by looping through and printing each line as follows:

```
> data.each_line { |line|
>       p line
> }
```

This returns the complete HTML source of the page confirming we have successfully scraped the New York Times homepage. To see more things that we can do with our data object, we can call `data.methods`.

The next step is to parse our data object and for this we need Nokogiri. Because we have already installed the gem, we can import it with a simple require statement:

```
> require 'nokogiri'
```

Similar to when we required `open-uri`, we should get a response back:

```
=> true
```

With Nokogiri loaded we can create a `Nokogiri::HTML::Document` from our data object:

```
> doc = Nokogiri::HTML(data)
```

 We could also combine the scraping with this step by expressing our `doc` variable as `doc = Nokogiri::HTML(open http://nytimes.com)`.

This will respond with the complete Nokogiri node set which looks very similar to the HTML source.

We can now use our previous CSS selector to take advantage of Nokogiri's `at_css` method. The `at_css` method searches for the first node matching the CSS selector. Our other option would be to use the `css` method which returns a NodeSet with all instances matching the CSS selector.

Since this selector only occurs once in our source, sticking with the `at_css` method should be fine:

```
> doc.at_css('h2 a')
```

This returns a Nokogiri XML Element node that matches our selector. If we look hard enough, we should see the headline within the response:

```
=> #<Nokogiri::XML::Element:0x3ff4161ab84c name="a" attributes=[#<Noko
giri::XML::Attr:0x3ff4161ab7e8 name="href" value="http://www.nytimes.
com/2013/06/10/us/former-cia-worker-says-he-leaked-surveillance-data.
html?hp">] children=[#<Nokogiri::XML::Text:0x3ff4161ab3b0 "\nEx-Worker
at\nC.I.A. Says He\nLeaked Data on\nSurveillance">]>
```

We can now make use of another Nokogiri method, `content`, to extract the text from the node.

```
> doc.at_css('h2 a').content
=> "\nEx-Worker at\nC.I.A. Says He\nLeaked Data on\nSurveillance"
```

Press the up arrow on your keyboard to cycle through your IRB history. This makes it especially easy to append another method on your last call.

And there we have the top headline from The New York Times. \n are line feeds marking new lines in the source. Because we now have a Ruby string, we can use the `gsub` method to clean it up with a simple search and replace. We can chain that to a `strip` method and remove any extra whitespace surrounding the string:

```
> doc.at_css('h2 a').content.gsub(/\n/," ").strip
=> "Ex-Worker at C.I.A. Says He Leaked Data on Surveillance"
```

Goal one complete! We now have the parsed text from the top headline stored in a variable.

That leaves the URL for the headline. The URL is located within the `href` attribute of the link. Nokogiri provides a `get_attribute` method which can easily extract the contents of an attribute:

```
> doc.at_css('h2 a').get_attribute('href')
=> "http://www.nytimes.com/2013/06/10/us/former-cia-worker-says-he-
leaked-surveillance-data.html?hp"And there we have the link.
```

You can also access an attribute using the `[:attr-name]` shortcut, for example `doc.at_css('h2 a')[:href]`.

You should see there is certain fluidity between research and explore. You analyze the DOM and come up with theories about which selectors you can use and then test those theories in the REPL.

You could just write code in a text editor and execute, but you don't get the same instantaneous feedback. Additionally, you will often find your resulting text or value requires some additional cleanup like we performed with the `gsub` and `strip` method. The REPL is a great place to play with these kinds of operations and investigate options.

If you like working within IRB, there is another project out there that is essentially a turbo-charged version called **Pry** (`http://pry.github.com`). It's a little advanced, so proceed with caution, but there's no reason you cannot have both running on your system.

Step 3 – write

We have our goal and our hypothesis. We've shown our hypothesis to be true. We have some sample code to execute our hypothesis. Now, it's time to write our Ruby script:

```ruby
# include the required libraries
require 'open-uri'
require 'nokogiri'

# scrape the web page
data = open('http://nytimes.com')

# create a Nokogiri HTML Document from our data
doc = Nokogiri::HTML(data)

# parse the top headline and clean it up
ny_times_headline = doc.at_css('h2 a').content.gsub(/\n/," ").strip

# parse the link for the top headline
ny_times_link = doc.at_css('h2 a').get_attribute('href')

# output the parsed data
p ny_times_headline
p ny_times_link
```

Let's give it a shot. Fire up your terminal and run:

```
$ ruby quickstart.rb
```

You should see the current top headline and link from The New York Times:

```
"Ex-Worker at C.I.A. Says He Leaked Data on Surveillance"
"http://www.nytimes.com/2013/06/10/us/former-cia-worker-says-he-leaked-
surveillance-data.html?hp"
```

Excellent! Our script is working. There is one more part we need to address for this to be a proper Ruby application and that is dependency management.

Our application requires a dependency, the Nokogiri gem. Our program only has one dependency. It is not a huge deal to expect another developer to look at the source and manually install Nokogiri, but to be a good citizen in the Ruby community we should manage our dependencies.

Bundler is the standard for managing dependencies in Ruby. To get started, create a file called Gemfile in the same directory as your script.

We now need to add two lines to our `Gemfile`.

```
source 'http://rubygems.org'
gem 'nokogiri'
```

The first line tells the bundler where to look for the gem. The second line tells bundler which gem to install. If you wanted to add another dependency, you could simply add another gem line:

```
gem 'another_required_gem'
```

With our gem file in place, you, or anyone else can install all required dependencies within the directory by running:

```
$ bundle install
Fetching gem metadata from https://rubygems.org/.........
Fetching gem metadata from https://rubygems.org/..
Resolving dependencies...
Using mini_portile (0.5.0)
Using nokogiri (1.6.0)
Using bundler (1.3.5)
Your bundle is complete!
```

Our dependency management is working!

Step 4 – extend

Technically we aren't done. We have our Ruby script that uses Nokogiri to extract a link to the top headline, but our broader goal was to create a news aggregation website. The easiest way to do this is with **Sinatra** (`http://www.sinatrarb.com/`). Sinatra provides a simple web wrapper for our script.

The Sinatra homepage is shown in the following screenshot:

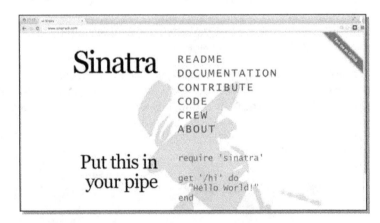

Sinatra is a Ruby gem. Rather than installing it from the command line, let's add it to our `Gemfile`:

```
source 'http://rubygems.org'
gem 'nokogiri'
gem 'sinatra'
```

To get all our dependencies installed, from the command line run:

$ bundle install

Your bundle is complete!

Sinatra is now installed.

This is not a Sinatra tutorial, but I think Sinatra is easy enough that you can follow along with the following commented source to see how the simple interaction with Sinatra and Nokogiri works:

```
# include the required libraries
require 'open-uri'
require 'nokogiri'
# add sinatra to the list
require 'sinatra'

# scrape the web page
data = open('http://nytimes.com')

# create a Nokogiri HTML Document from our data
doc = Nokogiri::HTML(data)

# parse the top headline and clean it up
ny_times_headline = doc.at_css('h2 a').content.gsub(/\n/," ").strip

# parse the link for the top headline
ny_times_link = doc.at_css('h2 a').get_attribute('href')

# create a HTML string we can send to the browser
# this first line is throw away wrapping the name of our newly
launched service
# inside a h1 tag
html = "<h1>Nokogiri News Service</h1>"
# here we append a link to the previous HTML using our parsed data
html += "<h2>Top Story: <a href=\"#{ny_times_link}\">#{ny_times_
headline}</a></h2>"

# this tells sinatra to respond to a request for the root document
get '/' do
  # send our HTML to the browser
  html
end
```

We can now spin up our web server by running the following script:

```
$ ruby quickstart_extend.rb
[2013-06-10 19:09:46] INFO  WEBrick 1.3.1
[2013-06-10 19:09:46] INFO  ruby 1.9.3 (2012-04-20) [x86_64-darwin12.2.1]
== Sinatra/1.4.3 has taken the stage on 4567 for development with backup
from WEBrick
[2013-06-10 19:09:46] INFO  WEBrick::HTTPServer#start: pid=6159 port=4567
```

This tells us the WEBrick server, which Sinatra is based on, has launched and is running on port 4567. This means we can access our site at `http://localhost:4567`.

Our running news aggregation site is shown in the following screenshot:

If we look at our final Sinatra-enabled Nokogiri script without the comments, it is 12 lines long! In those 12 little lines, we scrape the homepage of The New York Times, parse the top headline and link, construct a HTML document, spin up a web server, and respond to a get request at the root with our dynamic news service. That's why people like Ruby, and Nokogiri is one of the most downloaded gems.

Don't stop here, extend further and add additional sources. Read through the following top features to get more ideas on how to use the excellent Nokogiri gem.

Top 13 features you need to know about

Nokogiri is a pretty simple and straightforward gem. In the coming few pages we will take a more in-depth look at the most important methods, along with a few useful Ruby methods to take your parsing skills to the next level.

The css method

css(rules) —> NodeSet

The css method searches self for nodes matching CSS rules and returns an iterable NodeSet. Self is a Nokogiri::HTML::Document. In contrast to the at_css method used in the quick start project, the css method returns all nodes that match the CSS rules. The at_css method only returns the first node.

The following is a css method example:

```
# import nokogiri to parse and open-uri to scrape
require 'nokogiri'
require 'open-uri'

# create a new Nokogiri HTML document from the scraped URL
doc = Nokogiri::HTML(open('http://nytimes.com'))

# get all the h3 headings
doc.css('h3')

# get all the paragraphs
doc.css('p');

# get all the unordered lists
doc.css('ul')

# get all the section/category list items
doc.css('.navigationHomeLede li')
```

There is no explicit output from this code.

For more information refer to the site:

```
http://nokogiri.org/Nokogiri/XML/Node.html#method-i-css
```

The length method

length —> int

The `length` method returns the number of objects in self. Self is an array. `length` is one of the standard methods included with Ruby and is not Nokogiri-specific. It is very useful in playing with Nokogiri NodeSets as they extend the array class, meaning you can call `length` on them. For example, you can use `length` to see how many nodes are matching your CSS rule when using the `css` method.

An example of the `length` method is as follows:

```ruby
# import nokogiri to parse and open-uri to scrape
require 'nokogiri'
require 'open-uri'

# create a new Nokogiri HTML document from the scraped URL
doc = Nokogiri::HTML(open('http://nytimes.com'))

# get all the h3 headings
h3_count = doc.css('h3').length
puts "h3 count #{h3_count}"

# get all the paragraphs
p_count = doc.css('p').length;
puts "p count #{p_count}"

# get all the unordered lists
ul_count = doc.css('ul').length;
puts "ul count #{ul_count}"

# get all the section/category list items
# size is an alias for length and may be used interchangeably
section_count = doc.css('.navigationHomeLede li').size;
puts "section count #{section_count}"
Run the above code to see the counts.
$ ruby length.rb
h3 count 7
p count 47
ul count 64
section count 13
```

Your counts will be different as this code is running against the live New York Times website.

I use this method most in the IRB shell during the exploration phase. Once you know how large the array is, you can also access individual nodes using the standard array selector:

```
> doc.css('h3')[2]
 => #<Nokogiri::XML::Element:0x3fd31ec696f8 name="h3" children=[
#<Nokogiri::XML::Element:0x3fd31ec693b0 name="a" attributes=[#<N
okogiri::XML::Attr:0x3fd31ec692c0 name="href" value="http://www.
nytimes.com/2013/06/25/world/europe/snowden-case-carries-a-cold-war-
aftertaste.html?hp">] children=[#<Nokogiri::XML::Text:0x3fd31ec68924
"\nSnowden Case Has Cold War Aftertaste">]>]>
```

For more information refer to the site:

```
http://ruby-doc.org/core-2.0/Array.html#method-i-length
```

The each method 1

each { |item| block } —> ary

The each method calls the block once for each element in self. Self is a Ruby enumerable object. This method is part of the Ruby standard library and not specific to Nokogiri.

The each method is useful to iterate over Nokogiri NodeSets:

```
# import nokogiri to parse and open-uri to scrape
require 'nokogiri'
require 'open-uri'

# create a new Nokogiri HTML document from the scraped URL
doc = Nokogiri::HTML(open('http://nytimes.com'))

# iterate through the h3 headings
doc.css('h3').each{ |h3|
  puts h3
}
```

Run the preceding code to see the following iteration:

```
$ each.rb
<h3><a href="http://dealbook.nytimes.com/2013/06/24/u-s-civil-charges-
against-corzine-are-seen-as-near/?hp">
Regulators Are Said
to Plan a Civil Suit
Against Corzine</a></h3>
```

```
<h3><a href="http://www.nytimes.com/2013/06/25/business/global/credit-
warnings-give-world-a-peek-into-chinas-secretive-banks.html?hp">
Credit Warnings
Expose China&acirc;&#128;&#153;s
Secretive Banks</a></h3>

...
```

Your output will differ as this is run against the live New York Times website. For more information refer to the site:

```
http://ruby-doc.org/core-2.0/Array.html#method-i-each
```

The each method 2

each { |key,value| block } —> ary

There is also a Nokogiri native `each` method which is called on a single node to iterate over name value pairs in that node. This isn't particularly useful, but we will take a look at an example to help avoid confusion.

The example is as follows:

```
# import nokogiri to parse and open-uri to scrape
require 'nokogiri'
require 'open-uri'

# create a new Nokogiri HTML document from the scraped URL
doc = Nokogiri::HTML(open('http://nytimes.com'))

# iterate through key value pairs of an individual node
# as we know, the css method returns an enumberable object
# so we can access a specific node using standard array syntax
doc.css('a')[4].each{ |node_name, node_value|
  puts "#{node_name}: #{node_value}"
}
```

This shows us the available attributes for the fifth link on the page:

```
$ nokogiri_each.rb
style: display: none;
id: clickThru4Nyt4bar1_xwing2
```

```
href: http://www.nytimes.com/adx/bin/adx_click.html?type=goto&opzn&p
age=homepage.nytimes.com/index.html&pos=Bar1&sn2=5b35bc29/49f095e7&
sn1=ab317851/c628eac9&camp=nyt2013_abTest_multiTest_anchoredAd_bar1_
part2&ad=bar1_abTest_hover&goto=https%3A%2F%2Fwww%2Enytimesathome%2Ecom%2
Fhd%2F205%3Fadxc%3D218268%26adxa%3D340400%26page%3Dhomepage.nytimes.com/
index.html%26pos%3DBar1%26campaignId%3D3JW4F%26MediaCode%3DWB7AA
```

Your output will differ as this is run against the live New York Times website.

For more information refer to the site:

```
http://nokogiri.org/Nokogiri/XML/Node.html#method-i-each
```

The content method

content —> string

The content method returns the text content of a node. This is how you parse content from a CSS selector. If you used the css method and have a NodeSet, you will need to iterate with the each method to extract the content of each node.

The example for the content method is as follows:

```
# import nokogiri to parse and open-uri to scrape
require 'nokogiri'
require 'open-uri'

# create a new Nokogiri HTML document from the scraped URL
doc = Nokogiri::HTML(open('http://nytimes.com'))

# iterate through the h3 headings
doc.css('h3').each{ |h3|
  # extract the content from the h3
  puts h3.content
}
```

Run the preceding code to see the h3 tags content:

```
$ content.rb
Regulators Are Said to Plan a Civil Suit Against Corzine
Credit Warnings Expose China's Secretive Banks
Affirmative Action Case Has Both Sides Claiming Victory
Back in the News, but Never Off U.S. Radar When Exercise Becomes an
Addiction
Lee Bollinger: A Long, Slow Drift From Racial Justice
```

Your output will differ as this is run against the live New York Times website.

For more information refer to the site:

```
http://nokogiri.org/Nokogiri/XML/Node.html#method-i-content
```

The at_css method

at_css(rules) —> node

The at_css method searches the document and returns the first node matching the CSS selector. This is useful when you know there is only one match in the DOM or the first match is fine. Because it is able to stop at the first match, at_css is faster than the naked css method. Additionally, you don't have to iterate over the object to access its properties.

The example is as follows:

```
# import nokogiri to parse and open-uri to scrape
require 'nokogiri'
require 'open-uri'

# create a new Nokogiri HTML document from the scraped URL
doc = Nokogiri::HTML(open('http://nytimes.com'))

# get the content of the title of the page
# because there is only one title, we can use at_css
puts doc.at_css('title').content
```

Run the preceding code to parse the title:

$ ruby at_css.rb

The New York Times - Breaking News, World News & Multimedia

Your output will likely be the same because it is unlikely that The New York Times has changed their title tag, but it is possible they have updated it.

For more information refer to the site:

```
http://nokogiri.org/Nokogiri/XML/Node.html#method-i-at_css
```

The xpath method

xpath(paths) —> NodeSet

The xpath method searches self for nodes matching XPath rules and returns an iterable NodeSet. Self is a Nokogiri::HTML::Document or Nokogiri::XML::Document. The xpath method returns all nodes that match the XPath rules. The at_xpath method only returns the first node.

An example use of the xpath method is as follows:

```
# import nokogiri to parse and open-uri to scrape
require 'nokogiri'
require 'open-uri'

# create a new Nokogiri HTML document from the scraped URL
doc = Nokogiri::HTML(open('http://nytimes.com'))

# get all the h3 headings
h3_count = doc.xpath('//h3').length
puts "h3 count #{h3_count}"

# get all the paragraphs
p_count = doc.xpath('//p').length;
puts "p count #{p_count}"

# get all the unordered lists
ul_count = doc.xpath('//ul').length;
puts "ul count #{ul_count}"

# get all the section/category list items
# note this rule is substantially different from the CSS.
# *[@class="navigationHomeLede"] says to find any node
# with the class attribute = navigationHomeLede.  We then
# have to explicitly search for an unordered list before
# searching for list elements.
section_count = doc.xpath('//*[@class="navigationHomeLede"]/ul/li').
size;
puts "section count #{section_count}"
```

Run the preceding code to see the counts:

```
$ xpath.rb
h3 count 7
p count 47
ul count 64
section count 13
```

Your counts will differ as this code is running against the live New York Times website, but your counts should be consistent with using the css method.

For more information refer to the site:

```
http://nokogiri.org/Nokogiri/XML/Node.html#method-i-xpath
```

The at_xpath method

at_xpath(paths) —> node

The at_xpath method searches the document and returns the first node matching the XPath selector. This is useful when you know there is only one match in the DOM or the first match is fine. Because it is able to stop at the first match, at_xpath is faster than the naked xpath method. Additionally, you don't have to iterate over the object to access its properties.

An example for the at_xpath method is as follows:

```
# import nokogiri to parse and open-uri to scrape
require 'nokogiri'
require 'open-uri'

# create a new Nokogiri HTML document from the scraped URL
doc = Nokogiri::HTML(open('http://nytimes.com'));

# get the content of the title of the page
# because there is only one title, we can use at_css
puts doc.at_xpath('//title').content
```

Run the preceding code to parse the title:

$ ruby at_xpath.rb

The New York Times - Breaking News, World News & Multimedia

Your output will likely be the same because it is unlikely that The New York Times has changed their title tag, but it is possible they have updated it. Your output however should be the same as at_css.

For more information refer to the site:

http://nokogiri.org/Nokogiri/XML/Node.html#method-i-at_xpath

The to_s method

to_s —> string

The to_s method turns self into a string. If self is an HTML document, to_s returns HTML. If self is an XML document, to_s returns XML. This is useful in an IRB session where you want to examine the source of a node to determine how to craft your selector or need the raw HTML for your project.

An example of to_s is as follows:

```
# import nokogiri to parse and open-uri to scrape
require 'nokogiri'
```

```
require 'open-uri'

# create a new Nokogiri HTML document from the scraped URL
doc = Nokogiri::HTML(open('http://nytimes.com'))

# get the HTML for the top story link
# if you remember from the quick start, there is only one
# of these on the page, so we can us at_css to target.
puts doc.at_css('h2 a').to_s
```

Run the preceding code to see the HTML:

$ ruby to_s.rb

<a href="http://www.nytimes.com/2013/06/26/us/politics/obama-plan-to-cut-greenhouse-gases.html?hp">President to Outline Plan on Greenhouse Gas Emissions</a>

Your output will differ as this is run against the live New York Times website, but you should be able to confirm this is indeed the top headline by visiting http://www.nytimes.com in your browser.

For more information refer to the site:

http://nokogiri.org/Nokogiri/XML/Node.html#method-i-to_s

This concludes the base methods you will need to interact with Nokogiri for your scraping and parsing projects. You now know how to target specific content with CSS or XPath selectors, iterate through NodeSets, and extract their content. Next, we will go over a few tips and tricks that will help you should you get into a bind with your Nokogiri project.

Spoofing browser agents

When you request a web page, you send metainformation along with your request in the form of headers. One of these headers, User-agent, informs the web server which web browser you are using. By default open-uri, the library we are using to scrape, will report your browser as Ruby.

There are two issues with this. First, it makes it very easy for an administrator to look through their server logs and see if someone has been scraping the server. Ruby is not a standard web browser. Second, some web servers will deny requests that are made by a nonstandard browsing agent.

We are going to spoof our browser agent so that the server thinks we are just another Mac using Safari.

An example is as follows:

```
# import nokogiri to parse and open-uri to scrape
require 'nokogiri'
require 'open-uri'

# this string is the browser agent for Safari running on a Mac
browser = 'Mozilla/5.0 (Macintosh; Intel Mac OS X 10_8_4)
AppleWebKit/536.30.1 (KHTML, like Gecko) Version/6.0.5
Safari/536.30.1'

# create a new Nokogiri HTML document from the scraped URL and pass in
the
# browser agent as a second parameter
doc = Nokogiri::HTML(open('http://nytimes.com', browser))

# you can now go along with your request as normal
# you will show up as just another safari user in the logs
puts doc.at_css('h2 a').to_s
```

Caching

It's important to remember that every time we scrape content, we are using someone else's server's resources. While it is true that we are not using any more resources than a standard web browser request, the automated nature of our requests leave the potential for abuse.

In the previous examples we have searched for the top headline on The New York Times website. What if we took this code and put it in a loop because we always want to know the latest top headline? The code would work, but we would be launching a mini **denial of service** (**DOS**) attack on the server by hitting their page potentially thousands of times every minute.

Many servers, Google being one example, have automatic blocking set up to prevent these rapid requests. They ban IP addresses that access their resources too quickly. This is known as rate limiting.

To avoid being rate limited and in general be a good netizen, we need to implement a caching layer. Traditionally in a large app this would be implemented with a database. That's a little out of scope for this book, so we're going to build our own caching layer with a simple TXT file. We will store the headline in the file and then check the file modification date to see if enough time has passed before checking for new headlines.

Start by creating the cache.txt file in the same directory as your code:

```
$ touch cache.txt
```

We're now ready to craft our caching solution:

```ruby
# import nokogiri to parse and open-uri to scrape
require 'nokogiri'
require 'open-uri'

# set how long in minutes until our data is expired
# multiplied by 60 to convert to seconds
expiration = 1 * 60

# file to store our cache in
cache = "cache.txt"

# Calculate how old our cache is by subtracting it's modification time
# from the current time.

# Time.new gets the current time
# The mtime methods gets the modification time on a file
cache_age = Time.new - File.new(cache).mtime

# if the cache age is greater than our expiration time
if cache_age > expiration
  # our cache has expire
  puts "cache has expired. fetching new headline"

  # we will now use our code from the quick start to
  # snag a new headline

  # scrape the web page
  data = open('http://nytimes.com')

  # create a Nokogiri HTML Document from our data
  doc = Nokogiri::HTML(data)

  # parse the top headline and clean it up
  headline = doc.at_css('h2 a').content.gsub(/\n/," ").strip

  # we now need to save our new headline
  # the second File.open parameter "w" tells Ruby to overwrite
  # the old file
  File.open(cache, "w") do |file|
    # we then simply puts our text into the file
    file.puts headline
```

```
        end

    puts "cache updated"

  else
    # we should use our cached copy
    puts "using cached copy"
    # read cache into a string using the read method
    headline = IO.read("cache.txt")
  end

    puts "The top headline on The New York Times is ..."
    puts headline
```

Our cache is set to expire in one minute, so assuming it has been one minute since you created your cache.txt file, let's fire up our Ruby script:

$ ruby cache.rb

cache has expired. fetching new headline

cache updated

The top headline on The New York Times is ...

Supreme Court Invalidates Key Part of Voting Rights Act

If we run our script again before another minute passes, it should use the cached copy:

$ ruby cache.rb

using cached copy

The top headline on The New York Times is ...

Supreme Court Invalidates Key Part of Voting Rights Act

SSL

By default, open-uri does not support scraping a page with SSL. This means any URL that starts with https will give you an error. We can get around this by adding one line below our require statements:

```
# import nokogiri to parse and open-uri to scrape
require 'nokogiri'
require 'open-uri'

# disable SSL checking to allow scraping
OpenSSL::SSL::VERIFY_PEER = OpenSSL::SSL::VERIFY_NONE
```

Mechanize

Sometimes you need to interact with a page before you can scrape it. The most common examples are logging in or submitting a form. Nokogiri is not set up to interact with pages. Nokogiri doesn't even scrape or download the page. That duty falls on open-uri. If you need to interact with a page, there is another gem you will have to use: Mechanize.

Mechanize is created by the same team as Nokogiri and is used for automating interactions with websites. Mechanize includes a functioning copy of Nokogiri.

To get started, install the mechanize gem:

```
$ gem install mechanize
Successfully installed mechanize-2.7.1
```

We're going to recreate the code sample from the installation where we parsed the top Google results for "packt", except this time we are going to start by going to the Google home page and submitting the search form:

```
# mechanize takes the place of Nokogiri and open-uri
require 'mechanize'

# create a new mechanize agent
# think of this as launching your web browser
agent = Mechanize.new

# open a URL in your agent / web browser
page = agent.get('http://google.com/')

# the google homepage has one big search box
# if you inspect the HTML, you will find a form with the name 'f'
# inside of the form you will find a text input with the name 'q'
google_form = page.form('f')

# tell the page to set the q input inside the f form to 'packt'
google_form.q = 'packt'

# submit the form
page = agent.submit(google_form)

# loop through an array of objects matching a CSS
# selector. mechanize uses the search method instead of
# xpath or css. search supports xpath and css
# you can use the search method in Nokogiri too if you
# like it
page.search('h3.r').each do |link|
  # print the link text
  puts link.content
end
```

Now execute the Ruby script and you should see the titles for the top results:

```
$ ruby mechanize.rb
Packt Publishing: Home
Books
Latest Books
Login/register
PacktLib
Support
Contact
Packt - Wikipedia, the free encyclopedia
Packt Open Source (PacktOpenSource) on Twitter
Packt Publishing (packtpub) on Twitter
Packt Publishing | LinkedIn
Packt Publishing | Facebook
```

For more information refer to the site:

```
http://mechanize.rubyforge.org/
```

People and places you should get to know

If you need help with Nokogiri, here are some people and places that will prove invaluable.

Official sites

The following are the sites you can refer:

✦ Homepage and documentation: `http://nokogiri.org`

✦ Source code: `https://github.com/sparklemotion/nokogiri/`

Articles and tutorials

The top five Nokogiri resources are as follows:

✦ Nokogiri History, Present, and Future presentation slides from Nokogiri co-author *Mike Dalessio*: `http://bit.ly/nokogiri-goruco-2013`

✦ In-depth tutorial covering Ruby, Nokogiri, Sinatra, and Heroku complete with 90 minute behind-the-scenes screencast written by me: `http://hunterpowers.com/data-scraping-and-more-with-ruby-nokogiri-sinatra-and-heroku`

✦ RailsCasts episode 190: Screen Scraping with Nokogiri – an excellent Nokogiri quick start video: `http://railscasts.com/episodes/190-screen-scraping-with-nokogiri`

✦ Mechanize – an excellent Mechanize quick start video: `http://railscasts.com/episodes/191-mechanize RailsCasts episode 191`

✦ Nokogiri co-author *Mike Dalessio's* blog: `http://blog.flavorjon.es`

Community

The community sites are as follows:

✦ Listserve: `http://groups.google.com/group/nokogiri-talk`

✦ GitHub: `https://github.com/sparklemotion/nokogiri/`

✦ Wiki: `http://github.com/sparklemotion/nokogiri/wikis`

✦ Known issues: `http://github.com/sparklemotion/nokogiri/issues`

✦ Stackoverflow: `http://stackoverflow.com/search?q=nokogiri`

Twitter

Nokogiri leaders on Twitter are:

- ✦ Nokogiri co-author *Mike Dalessio*: @flavorjones
- ✦ Nokogiri co-author *Aaron Patterson*: @tenderlove
- ✦ Me: @TheHunter
- ✦ For more information on open source, follow Packt Publishing: @PacktOpenSource

**Thank you for buying
Instant Nokogiri**

About Packt Publishing

Packt, pronounced 'packed', published its first book "*Mastering phpMyAdmin for Effective MySQL Management*" in April 2004 and subsequently continued to specialize in publishing highly focused books on specific technologies and solutions.

Our books and publications share the experiences of your fellow IT professionals in adapting and customizing today's systems, applications, and frameworks. Our solution based books give you the knowledge and power to customize the software and technologies you're using to get the job done. Packt books are more specific and less general than the IT books you have seen in the past. Our unique business model allows us to bring you more focused information, giving you more of what you need to know, and less of what you don't.

Packt is a modern, yet unique publishing company, which focuses on producing quality, cutting-edge books for communities of developers, administrators, and newbies alike. For more information, please visit our website: www.packtpub.com.

Writing for Packt

We welcome all inquiries from people who are interested in authoring. Book proposals should be sent to author@packtpub.com. If your book idea is still at an early stage and you would like to discuss it first before writing a formal book proposal, contact us; one of our commissioning editors will get in touch with you.

We're not just looking for published authors; if you have strong technical skills but no writing experience, our experienced editors can help you develop a writing career, or simply get some additional reward for your expertise.

PUBLISHING

Ruby and MongoDB Web Development Beginner's Guide

ISBN: 978-1-84951-502-3   Paperback: 332 pages

Create dynamic web applications by combining the power of Ruby and MongoDB

1. Step-by-step instructions and practical examples to creating web applications with Ruby and MongoDB

2. Learn to design the object model in a NoSQL way

3. Create objects in Ruby and map them to MongoDB

Cloning Internet Applications with Ruby

ISBN: 978-1-84951-106-3   Paperback: 336 pages

Make your own TinyURL, Twitter, Flickr, or Facebook using Ruby

1. Build your own custom social networking, URL shortening, and photo sharing websites using Ruby

2. Deploy and launch your custom high-end web applications

3. Learn what makes popular social networking sites such as Twitter and Facebook tick

4. Understand features of some of the most famous photo sharing and social networking websites

Please check **www.PacktPub.com** for information on our titles

Instant RubyMotion App Development

ISBN: 978-1-84969-652-4   Paperback: 54 pages

A jump start to quickly learn how to program iOS applicatons with the elegance and simplicity of Ruby

1. Learn something new in an Instant! A short, fast, focused guide delivering immediate results

2. Learn the structure of iPhone and iPad applications

3. Discover how to simplify iOS apps with Ruby

4. Get to grips with how to leverage Ruby libraries to quickly and efficiently write apps

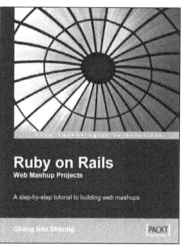

Ruby on Rails Web Mashup Projects

ISBN: 978-1-84719-393-3   Paperback: 272 pages

A step-by-step tutorial to building web mashups

1. Learn about web mashup applications and mashup plug-ins

2. Create practical real-life web mashup projects step-by-step

3. Access and mash up many different APIs with Ruby and Ruby on Rails

Please check **www.PacktPub.com** for information on our titles